TOP SOCCER TOURNAMENTS AROUND THE WORLD

Mauricio Velázquez de León

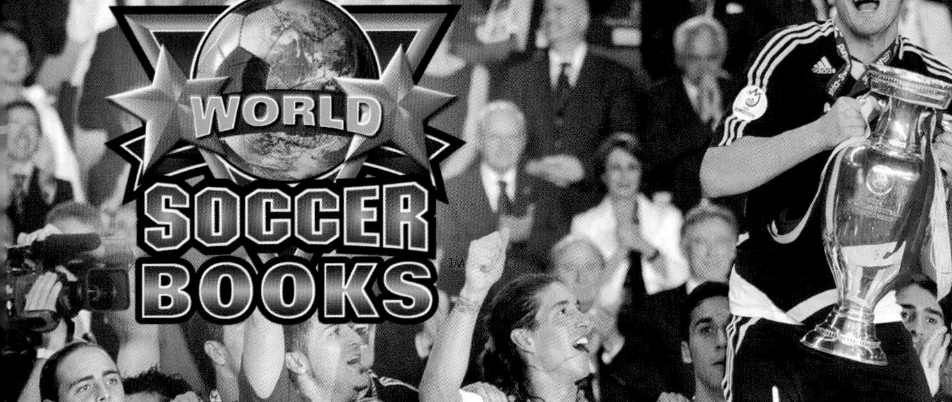

rosen publishing's
rosen central
New York

Published in 2010 by The Rosen Publishing Group, Inc.
29 East 21st Street, New York, NY 10010

First Edition

Library of Congress Cataloging-in-Publication Data

Velázquez de León, Mauricio
Top soccer tournaments around the world / Mauricio Velazquez de Leon.–1st ed.
p. cm.–(World soccer books)
Includes bibliographical references and index.
ISBN 978-1-4358-9140-1 (library binding)
ISBN 978-1-61532-877-2 (pbk)
ISBN 978-1-61532-878-9 (6 pack)
1. Soccer–Juvenile literature. 2. Soccer–Tournaments–Juvenile literature. I. Title.
GV943.25.V45 2010
796.334–dc22

2009021859

Manufactured in China

CPSIA Compliance Information: Batch #HW10YA: For Further Information contact Rosen Publishing, New York, New York at 1-800-237-9932

On the cover: Top: The German national team celebrates after winning the Women's World Cup in 2007. Bottom: Iker Casillas, captain of the Spanish national team, lifts the 2008 EURO Cup.

CONTENTS

INTRODUCTION

The World Cup is a truly global phenomenon. Besides the Olympics, no other athletic competition captures the imagination of so many people, in so many different places, in such an intense way.

Before the World Cup became soccer's main international competition, every region of the world had its own soccer tournament. These tournaments encouraged soccer rivalries among nations, and fed the passion that makes soccer the most popular sport on the planet. Fourteen years before the first World Cup, South American nations were already competing against one another for soccer glory. Some soccer rivalries are more than one hundred years old. For instance, the enmity between Scottish and English soccer fans dates back to 1872, when the first international soccer game was played. In many ways, the success of the World Cup is due to these early matches and regional tournaments.

International soccer tournaments are administered by the Fédération Internationale de Football Association (FIFA), the umbrella organization for all things soccer. FIFA has organized world soccer into six organizations: the Asian Football Confederation (AFC), the Confédération Africaine de Football (CAF), the Confederation of North, Central America and Caribbean Association Football (CONCACAF), the Confederación Sudamericana de Fútbol (CONMEBOL), the Oceania Football Confederation (OFC), and the Union of European Football Associations (UEFA). Each of these organizations controls their own regional tournament. The structure of these tournaments resembles the World Cup, with qualifying rounds followed by a final round that is hosted by one or two countries. The success of the World Cup has led FIFA to create other worldwide tournaments focused on specific groups, such as youth teams. FIFA has also established the very successful FIFA Women's World Cup.

Fireworks commemorate the opening of the 2006 African Cup of Nations in Cairo, Egypt. Sixteen teams participated in the tournament.

CHAPTER 1

THE WORLD CUP

The World Cup is the most popular sporting event in the world. In the 2010 World Cup in South Africa, 204 countries signed for the qualifiers. Today, more nations are members of FIFA than the Olympic committee–or even the United Nations!

It is impossible to measure the passion of soccer fans and the hope that each country has for their national team. The sheer size and scope of the World Cup, however, gives us some insight into the scale of worldwide soccer enthusiasm. More than 715 million soccer fans watched the final match of the 2006 World Cup in Germany. The World Cup finals take place every four years and last for about a month, but the actual World Cup tournament begins three years before the finals. All 204 teams competing in the World Cup begin competing in the qualifying rounds. Since 1998, the World Cup finals have had thirty-two available spots. Virtually the entire planet is vying for these thirty-two spots, and as you might expect, the competition is fierce. However, it hasn't always been this way. When Uruguay hosted the first World Cup in 1930, few countries wanted to participate.

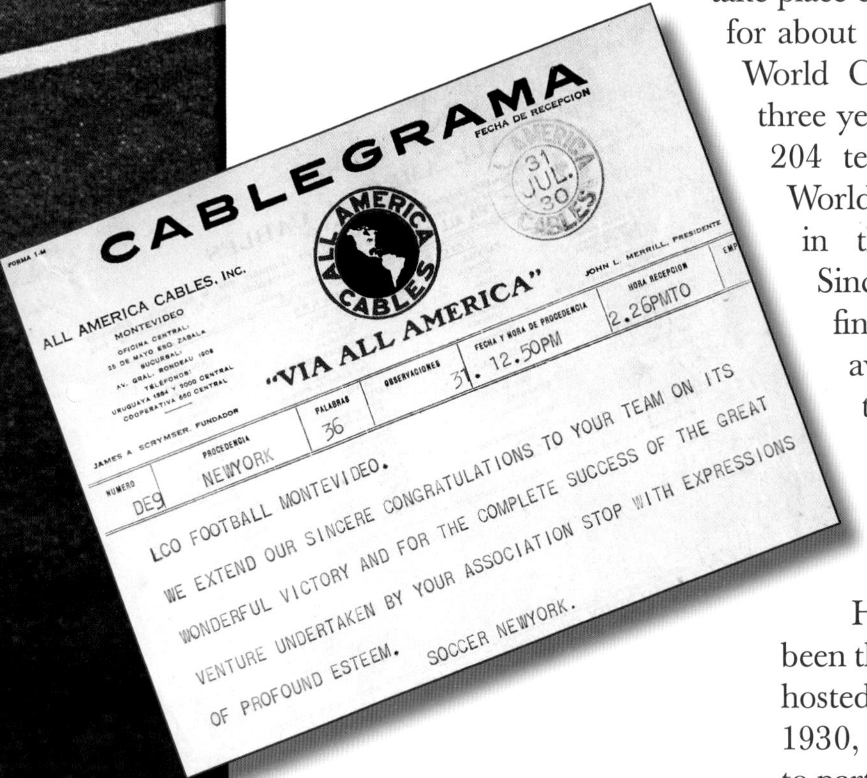
CABLEGRAMA
FECHA DE RECEPCION
FORMA 1-M
ALL AMERICA CABLES, INC.
MONTEVIDEO
OFICINA CENTRAL: 25 DE MAYO ESQ. ZABALA
SUCURSAL: AV. GRAL. RONDEAU 1906
TELEFONOS: URUGUAYA 1564 Y 2000 CENTRAL
COOPERATIVA 660 CENTRAL
JAMES A. SCRYMSER, FUNDADOR
JOHN L. MERRILL, PRESIDENTE
"VIA ALL AMERICA"
ALL AMERICA CABLES
31 JUL. 30

NUMERO	PROCEDENCIA	PALABRAS	OBSERVACIONES	FECHA Y HORA DE PROCEDENCIA	HORA RECEPCION
DE9	NEWYORK	36		31. 12.50PM	2.26PMTO

LCO FOOTBALL MONTEVIDEO.
WE EXTEND OUR SINCERE CONGRATULATIONS TO YOUR TEAM ON ITS WONDERFUL VICTORY AND FOR THE COMPLETE SUCCESS OF THE GREAT VENTURE UNDERTAKEN BY YOUR ASSOCIATION STOP WITH EXPRESSIONS OF PROFOUND ESTEEM. SOCCER NEWYORK.

The USA Soccer Federation sent this cablegram to the Uruguayan Football Association in July 1930, congratulating them on their victory in the first ever World Cup final.

ORIGINS OF THE WORLD CUP

FIFA was first established in 1904, with the goal of creating an international soccer

YEAR/HOST	WINNER	FINAL SCORE	RUNNER -UP
1930 URUGUAY	URUGUAY	4–2	ARGENTINA
1934 ITALY	ITALY	2–1	CZECHOSLOVAKIA
1938 FRANCE	ITALY	4–2	HUNGARY
1950 BRAZIL	URUGUAY	4–2	BRAZIL
1954 SWITZERLAND	WEST GERMANY	3–2	HUNGARY
1958 SWEDEN	BRAZIL	5–2	SWEDEN
1962 CHILE	BRAZIL	3–1	CZECHOSLOVAKIA
1966 ENGLAND	ENGLAND	4–2	WEST GERMANY
1970 MEXICO	BRAZIL	4–1	ITALY
1974 WEST GERMANY	WEST GERMANY	2–1	HOLLAND
1978 ARGENTINA	ARGENTINA	3–1	HOLLAND
1982 SPAIN	ITALY	3–1	WEST GERMANY
1986 MEXICO	ARGENTINA	3–2	WEST GERMANY
1990 ITALY	WEST GERMANY	1–0	ARGENTINA
1994 USA	BRAZIL	0–0 (3–2) *	ITALY
1998 FRANCE	FRANCE	3–0	BRAZIL
2002 KOREA/JAPAN	BRAZIL	2–0	GERMANY
2006 GERMANY	ITALY	1–1 (5–3) *	GERMANY

* GAME DECIDED IN A PENALTY SHOOT-OUT

competition. FIFA originally tried to create a global soccer tournament in 1906, but the idea didn't take off. However, when soccer became an Olympic sport, FIFA's president, Jules Rimet, decided to give the World Cup another try. In 1929, FIFA selected Uruguay to host the first World Cup tournament. Since Uruguay had won the gold medal in Olympic soccer in 1928, FIFA believed that the South American country deserved the honor of hosting.

Two months before the first World Cup tournament, however, no European countries had signed up to play. At that time, the trip from Europe to South America was long and expensive. Still, Rimet was determined to make the World Cup work. He talked Belgium, France, Romania, and Yugoslavia into coming from Europe. Nine more teams came from North and South America, including the United States. In total, thirteen teams participated. On July 13,

THE WORLD CUP

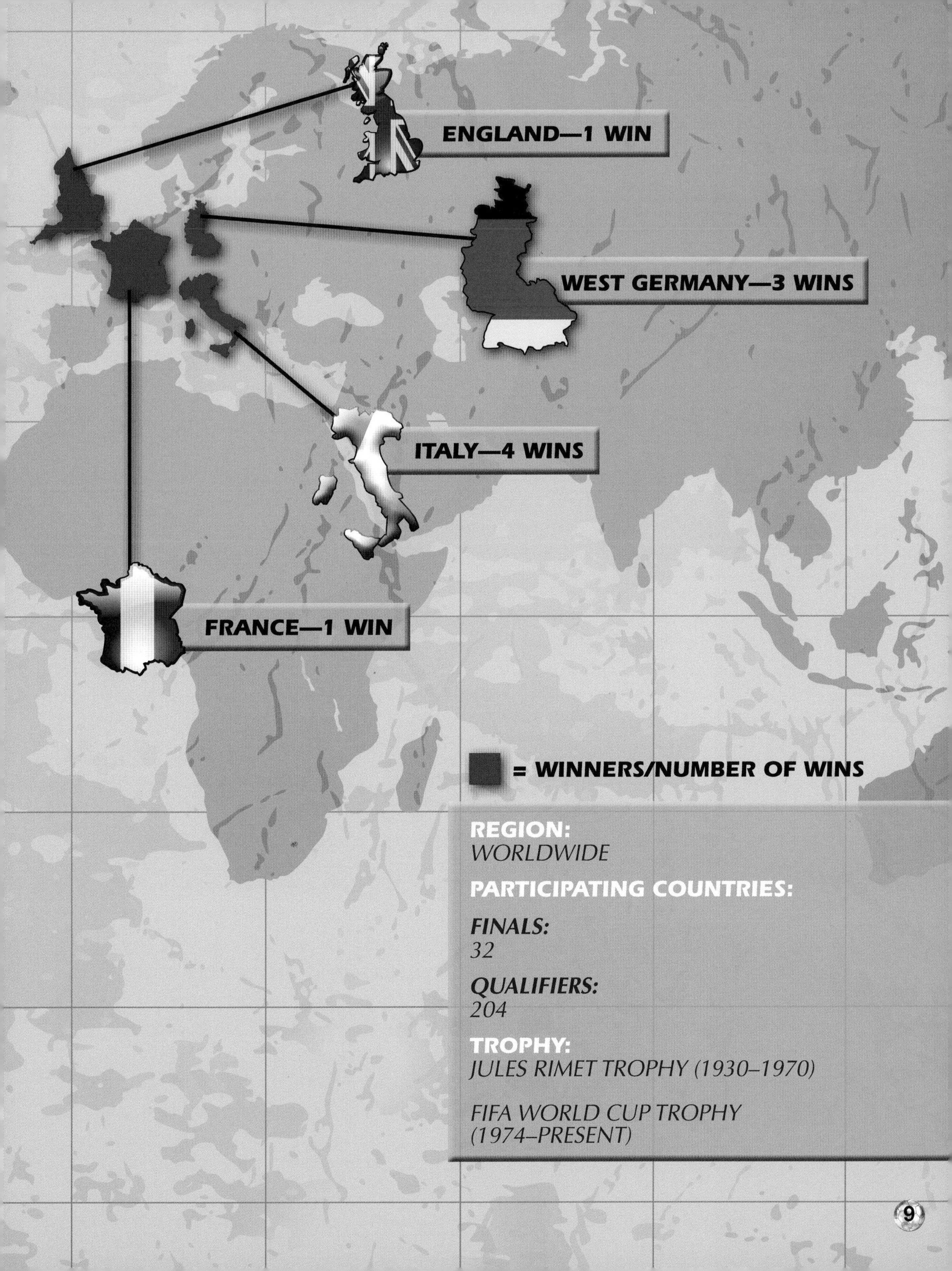
ENGLAND—1 WIN
WEST GERMANY—3 WINS
ITALY—4 WINS
FRANCE—1 WIN
= WINNERS/NUMBER OF WINS
REGION:
WORLDWIDE
PARTICIPATING COUNTRIES:
FINALS:
32
QUALIFIERS:
204
TROPHY:
JULES RIMET TROPHY (1930–1970)
FIFA WORLD CUP TROPHY
(1974–PRESENT)

1930, the national teams of France and Mexico played the first World Cup game in history. On July 30, 1930, Uruguay won a thrilling final game against Argentina, becoming the first World Cup champion.

AN EXCLUSIVE CLUB

With this victory, Uruguay became the first member of an exclusive club of World Cup winners. Since 1930, the World Cup has been held eighteen times, and only seven countries have won it. England and France have each won one final, and two-time winner Uruguay hasn't won since 1950. The other winners of the World Cup–Argentina, Brazil, Italy, and Germany–are generally considered to be the four superpowers of international soccer.

Italy became the first world soccer powerhouse after winning back-to-back tournaments in 1934 and 1938. The Italian team, known for having a strong defense and a talented midfield, saw its run interrupted by World War II. The war put a halt to all World Cup action until 1950. The Italians returned to glory in 1982, once again capturing the cup. Italy won its fourth title in 2006.

Although they are two-time World Cup champions, Argentina did not win a World Cup final until 1978. Argentina won its first trophy when playing at home. Famous for a blend of European style and South American skill, Argentina won its second title in 1986. Soccer legend Diego Armando Maradona, considered to be one of the greatest players in soccer history, was one of the keys to Argentina's 1986 victory.

Germany's soccer reputation has been built around its incredible consistency. Three-time champions West Germany won the World Cup in 1954, 1974, and 1990. (From 1949 to 1990, Germany was split into two countries: democratic West Germany and socialist East Germany. In 1990, the two countries were reunited.) Germany's most impressive feat may be the fact that it has made it to eight of the eighteen World Cup finals.

As remarkable as Germany's record is, the most impressive team in World Cup history is Brazil. Architects of a style known as "the beautiful game," Brazil won back-to-back championships in

Brazilian captain Cafu lifts the FIFA World Cup among his teammates after winning Brazil's fifth World Cup title in 2002 in Japan.

1958 and 1962. After winning the World Cup for a third time in 1970, it claimed the right to keep the Jules Rimet Trophy for life. Brazil won a fourth title in the 1994 World Cup, played on U.S. soil. In 2002, Brazil won a record-breaking fifth World Cup title.

WORLD CUP STARS

Soccer is a team sport, and the World Cup has had its share of renowned teams. Some of the most legendary include Hungary's "Magical Magyars" of the 1950s, the Dutch team of the 1970s, and the Brazilian team from 1954 to 1970. Great teams are powered by legendary players, many of whom have become heroes to soccer fans around the world.

There is no doubt that the success of the World Cup has much to do with a Brazilian player named Edson Arantes do Nascimento, known to soccer fans everywhere as Pelé. At the age of seventeen, Pelé scored two goals in the 1958 World Cup final to give Brazil its first title. Soccer fans were captivated by the sheer confidence and skill of the young superstar. Pelé played in four World Cups, helping to win three titles for Brazil. He was also named Player of the Century. Besides Pelé, no other footballer has so captivated the fans' imagination with his skill and ball control as Diego Armando Maradona, the talented midfielder who took Argentina to victory in the 1986 World Cup.

Many soccer stars might not have been world champions, but they certainly have a place in the history of the World Cup. One such player is French striker Just Fontaine. Fontaine scored thirteen goals throughout the 1958 World Cup, a record that has yet to be broken. Other World Cup superstars include Dutch luminary Johan Cruyff, a runner-up in the 1974 World Cup, and Mozambique-born striker Eusébio da Silva Ferreira (known simply as Eusébio) who played for Portugal in the 1960s and 1970s.

EXTRAORDINARY MATCHES

Out of the hundreds of games that have been played in the World Cup, several stand out as being completely extraordinary. The 1966 quarterfinal between Portugal and Korea is one of these matches. Twenty-five minutes into the first half, Korea lead the game 3–0. Against extraordinary odds, Portuguese star Eusébio staged a remarkable comeback by scoring four goals to send Portugal to the semifinals.

Another legendary game was the 1990 World Cup quarterfinal match between Cameroon and England. England scored first, but Cameroon's secret weapon, Roger

The mascot for the 2010 World Cup in South Africa is named Zakumi. South Africa is the first African country to host the World Cup tournament.

Milla, came off the bench, scoring to tie the match. Four minutes later, Milla assisted Eugène Ekéké, putting underdogs Cameroon in the lead. England scored again toward the end of the game, which went into overtime. Completely exhausted, both teams kept pressing for a win. Cameroon had several chances, but it was British striker Gary Lineker who decided the battle in a penalty kick.

Out of all these astounding matches, experts agree that the most extraordinary game in World Cup history was played on June 17, 1970, in Mexico City's Azteca Stadium. It was the semifinal game between Italy and West Germany and the two powerful soccer titans didn't disappoint. After Italy scored a goal, the German side pushed forward. In the sixty-seventh minute, German defender Franz Beckenbauer charged over an Italian player, falling dramatically on the field. Beckenbauer dislocated his right shoulder but didn't leave the field. Germany tied the game, sending it into the most memorable period of overtime in soccer history.

Beckenbauer led the German team with his arm in a sling strapped to his body. Gigi Riva was in charge of the Italian game. Germany took the lead, but Italy scored twice before the end of the first overtime period. It looked like Italy would advance to the final, but Germany returned when Gerd Müller scored a goal to tie the game. The German push was short-lived. Italian player Gianni Rivera scored the final goal of the match almost immediately. After playing intensely for 111 minutes, the German team was prepared to keep fighting, but their legs couldn't take it anymore. Italy won 4–3, and the match became known as the "Game of the Century."

THE WORLD CUP TODAY

The history of the World Cup continues to be written. FIFA's decision to give Japan and Korea the opportunity to cohost the cup for the first time in 2002, and the choice of South Africa to host the cup in 2010, making it the first World Cup to be played in Africa, demonstrate that there is still room for soccer to grow. All signs seem to suggest that soccer will continue to be the most popular sport on the planet for many more years.

CHAPTER 2
THE AFRICAN CUP OF NATIONS

Egypt, Ghana, and Cameroon are the major powers of the African Cup of Nations, the African soccer tournament that was established in 1957. The first cup was hosted by Sudan and was played between Egypt, Ethiopia, and Sudan. Egypt became the first African Cup of Nations champion after defeating Ethiopia in the finals.

The African Cup of Nations was to originally include a fourth nation: South Africa. A founding member of the Confédération Africaine de Football (African Football Confederation, or CAF), the country was disqualified from the African Cup of Nations after refusing to send a multiracial team. At the time, South Africa was a nation with a white ruling class that enforced the segregation of blacks

Cameroon's Samuel Eto'o, the all-time leading scorer in the history of the African Cup of Nations, controls the ball during a 2002 match against Egypt.

TEAM	TITLES/YEAR
ALGERIA	1 (1990)
CAMEROON	4 (1984, 1988, 2000, 2002)
CONGO	1 (1972)
CONGO DR	2 (1968, 1974)
CÔTE D'IVOIRE	1 (1992)
EGYPT	6 (1957, 1959, 1986, 1998, 2006, 2008)
ETHIOPIA	1 (1962)
GHANA	4 (1963, 1965, 1978, 1982)
MOROCCO	1 (1976)
NIGERIA	2 (1980, 1994)
SOUTH AFRICA	1 (1996)
SUDAN	1 (1970)
TUNISIA	1 (2004)

and whites. This policy was known as apartheid. South Africa did not return to the competition until 1996, when it ended apartheid.

Ghana became the first country to win three African Cup of Nations championships. It commanded back-to-back victories in 1963 and 1965 and claimed a third win in 1978. These three victories meant that Ghana gained the right to keep the Abdel Aziz Abdallah Salem Trophy for life. This trophy was named after the first CAF president.

WEST AFRICAN POWER

By the late 1960s, interest in the tournament had grown among the fifty-five members of the CAF. Since 1968, the tournament has been played every two years. Interest in the tournament has corresponded with the rapid rise of African teams and players on the world stage during the 1970s.

By the time the 1980 African Cup of Nations was held in Nigeria, the tournament had become one of the main events

THE AFRICAN CUP OF NATIONS

GHANA—4 WINS

CÔTE D'IVOIRE—1 WIN

= WINNERS/NUMBER OF WINS

NIGERIA—2 WINS

CAMEROON—4 WINS

REGION:
AFRICA

CONFEDERATION
CONFÉDÉRATION AFRICAINE DE FOOTBALL (CAF)

PARTICIPATING COUNTRIES:
16

TROPHY:
ABDEL AZIZ ABDALLAH SALEM TROPHY (UNTIL 1978)

TROPHY OF AFRICAN UNITY, AKA AFRICAN UNITY CUP (1980 TO 2000)

AFRICAN CUP TROPHY (FROM 2000)

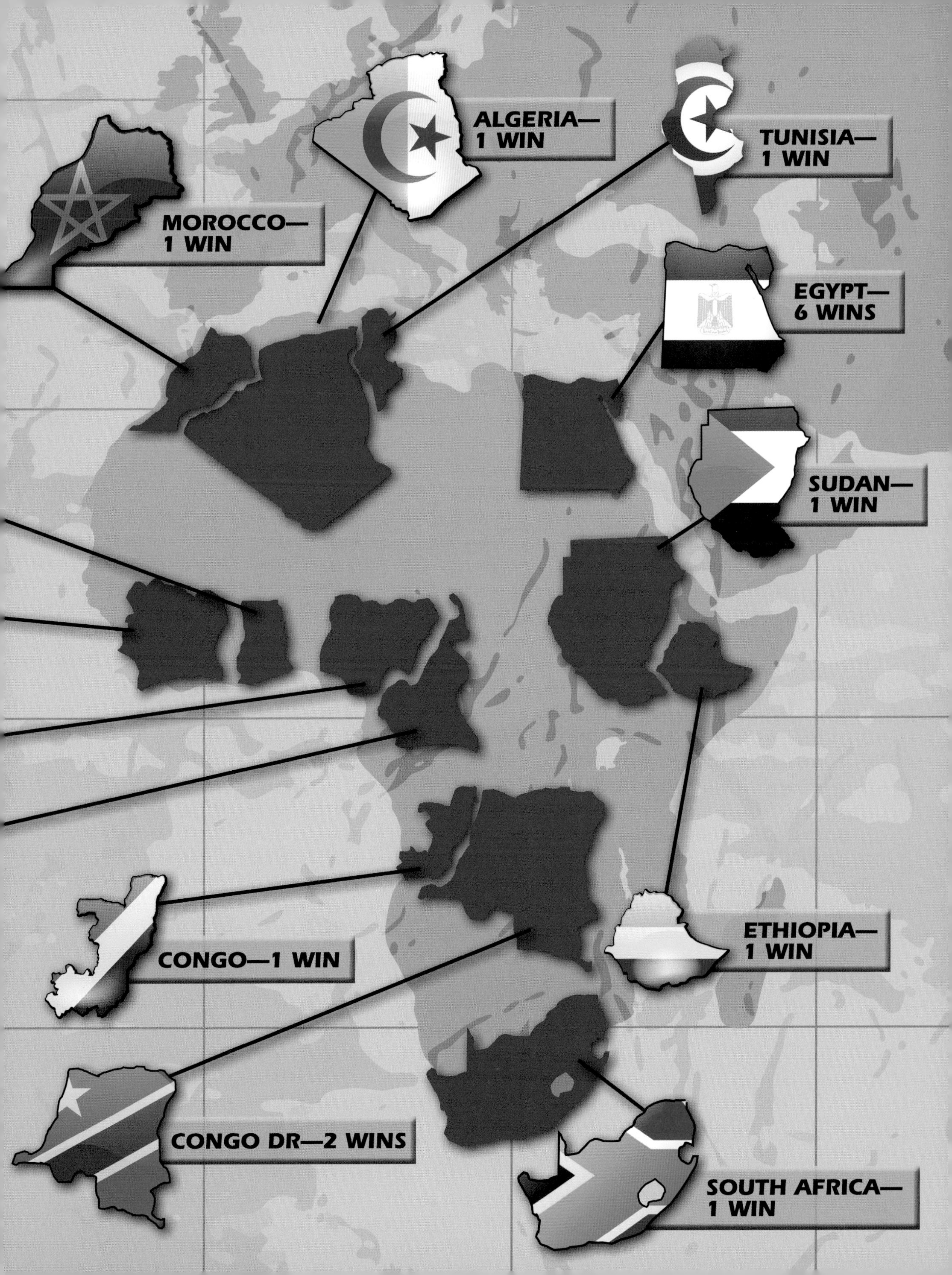
ALGERIA—
1 WIN
TUNISIA—
1 WIN
MOROCCO—
1 WIN
EGYPT—
6 WINS
SUDAN—
1 WIN
CONGO—1 WIN
ETHIOPIA—
1 WIN
CONGO DR—2 WINS
SOUTH AFRICA—
1 WIN

on the continent. Nigeria won the 1980 tournament at home, but perhaps more importantly, the nation successfully hosted the largest tournament to date. More than 730,000 soccer fans attended the games.

Ghana won its fourth African Cup of Nations in 1982, but Cameroon was the country that rose to dominate the rest of the decade. Cameroon beat Nigeria in 1984 and finished second four years later after failing to win against Egypt, the host of the tournament. Cameroon reached its third consecutive final in 1988, winning a second championship after beating Nigeria. Cameroon beat Nigeria in its third final match in 2000, wining the right to keep the Trophy of African Unity after becoming three-time African Cup champion.

THE CHAMPIONS OF NORTH AFRICA

Cameroon won its fourth title in 2002, tying Ghana and Egypt. Four years later, Egypt was ready to get back on top. Egypt hosted the cup in 2006, easily advancing to the final against Côte d'Ivoire. Winning the final itself, however, proved to be more difficult. After 120 minutes of exhausting play, Egypt won its fifth African Cup of Nations championship. Four years later, Egypt repeated its stellar performance in a spectacular tournament that produced ninety-nine goals, the highest-scoring African Cup of Nations ever. By defeating Cameroon in the final, Egypt won its sixth title and reaffirmed its position as the most successful team in Africa.

Egypt has won the African Cup of Nations six times. Here, Mohamed Zidan of Egypt dribbles the ball away from a Cameroonian defender in 2008.

CHAPTER 3

THE ASIAN CUP

The Asian Cup was held for the first time in 1956 in Hong Kong. Four countries competed in the finals: Israel, South Vietnam, Hong Kong, and the winners of the first championship, South Korea. Today, the tournament has developed into an extremely competitive event. The 2007 tournament was hosted by four nations: Indonesia, Malaysia, Thailand, and Vietnam. Twenty-four countries fought to qualify for the twelve available spots. The Asian Cup was held, uninterrupted, every four years until 2004. Because the cup was played the same year as the Summer Olympic Games and the European Football Championship, the AFC decided to move the tournament to

The television broadcast of the final game of the 2004 Asian Cup, where Japan faced off against China for the championship, was watched by 250 million people.

TEAM	TITLES/YEAR
IRAN	3 (1968, 1972, 1976)
IRAQ	1 (2007)
ISRAEL *	1 (1964)
JAPAN	3 (1992, 2000, 2004)
KUWAIT	1 (1980)
SAUDI ARABIA	3 (1984, 1988, 1996)
SOUTH KOREA	2 (1956, 1960)

* ISRAEL NO LONGER COMPETES IN THE AFC

a less crowded cycle. After 2004, the tournament was next held in 2007. It will continue to be held every four years.

Many of the countries that belong to the AFC have a tense political history. These regional conflicts have often shaped the way the Asian Cup is played. Israel, for instance, was accepted to FIFA in 1929 and joined the AFC in 1956. Israel hosted the Asian Cup in 1964, winning the trophy undefeated. Nevertheless, many Middle Eastern nations refused to compete against Israel. In the early 1970s, Israel was expelled from the AFC due to political pressure from Arab countries. For twenty years Israel was not affiliated with any confederation. In 1994, it was admitted to the UEFA.

ARAB NATIONS IN CHARGE

In 1968, Iran won the Asian Cup. At the time, soccer was banned in many Islamic nations for religious reasons. The Iranian team impressed the soccer world with a perfect record of four wins, including a final game against Israel. The Iranian team dominated the next two Asian Cups. Iran became the first country to get a hat trick in the tournament and achieved a historic run of seventeen undefeated games that ended with a defeat against Kuwait in the 1980 semifinals. After Iran's dominance of the cup ended, Saudia Arabia rose to power. Saudi Arabia won the cup in 1984, 1988, and 1996.

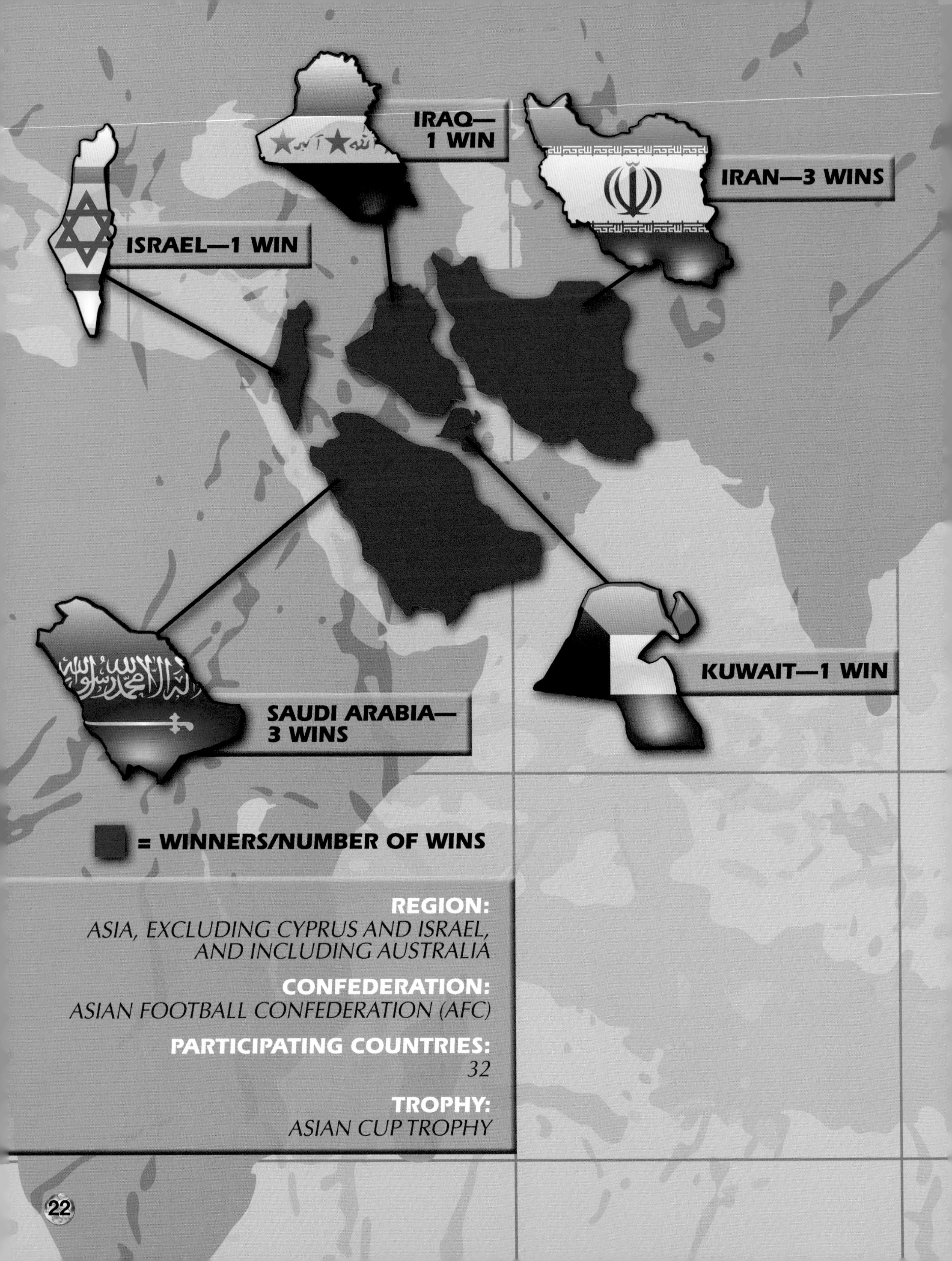

REGION:
ASIA, EXCLUDING CYPRUS AND ISRAEL, AND INCLUDING AUSTRALIA

CONFEDERATION:
ASIAN FOOTBALL CONFEDERATION (AFC)

PARTICIPATING COUNTRIES:
32

TROPHY:
ASIAN CUP TROPHY

THE ASIAN CUP

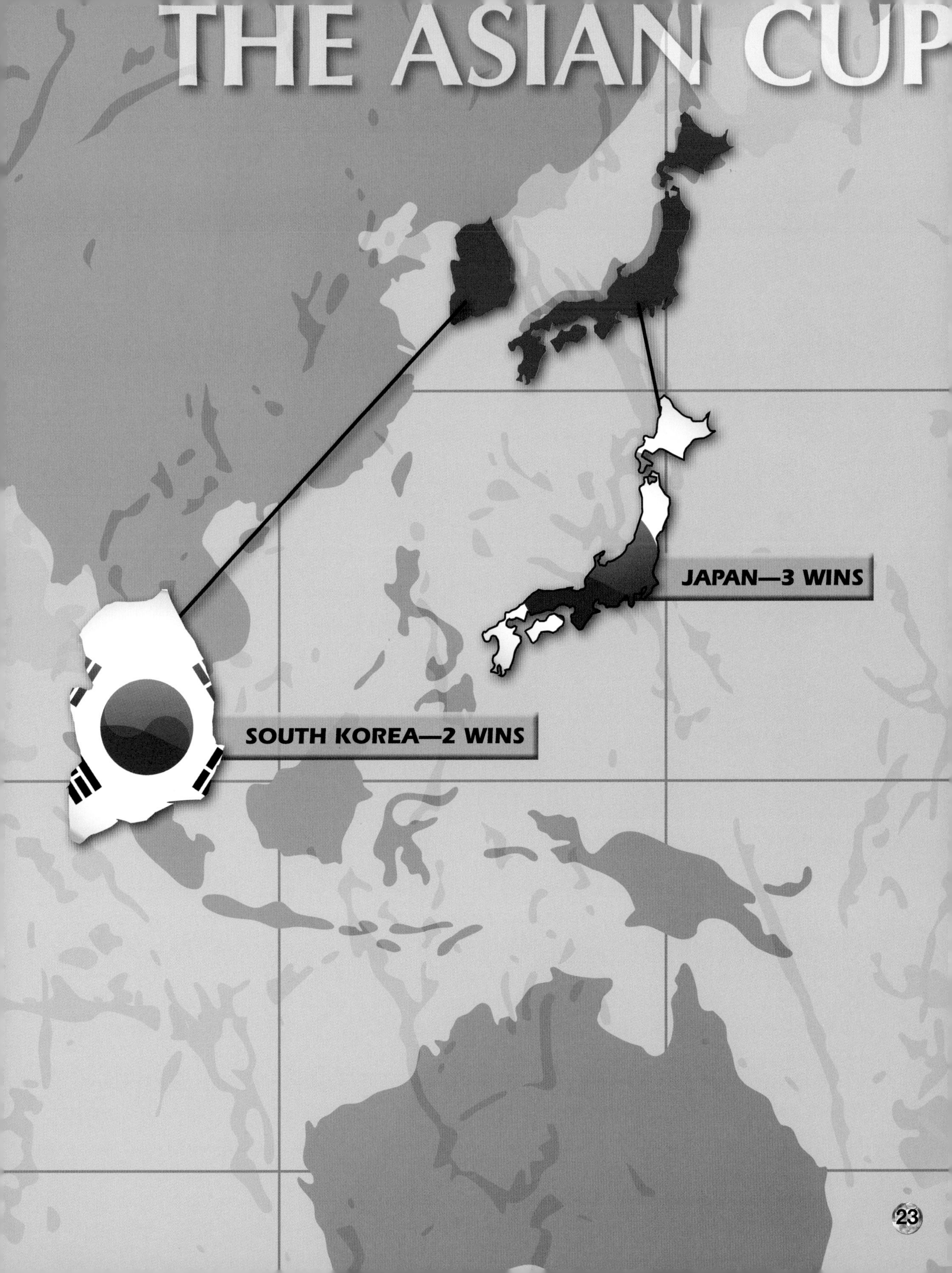

Iraqi team captain Younis Mahmoud celebrates after Iraq's victory in the 2007 Asian Cup final against Saudi Arabia.

The 1992 Asian Cup was hosted by Japan. This cup was much different from those that had come before, with on-field conflict taking center stage. During the sixteen matches, eight players were given red cards, and forty-nine received yellow cards. The Iranian national team was the main agitator of this conflict. Three of its players were given one-year bans, and two more were banned for a game. The battles on the field ended when Japan won the cup by defeating Saudi Arabia 1–0. During this game, five players were given yellow cards.

Four years later, the championship was held in the United Arab Emirates. This tournament saw a very different Iranian team, and in fact, the Iranians won the newly instituted Fair Play Award.

HISTORICAL TENSIONS

Japan became a repeat Asian Cup champion in the 2000 tournament, which was hosted by Lebanon. Four years later, Japan faced China in the most anticipated final in Asian Cup history. Playing at home, the Chinese squad reached the final after defeating all opponents. The two historical rivals faced each other in a tense match in front of 62,000 fans at Workers Stadium in Beijing. The game was watched by 250 million people on television, the largest audience ever for an Asian Cup game. Japan scored the first goal, but Chinese soccer legend Li Ming tied the game before halftime. Japan took control in the second half, and in the sixty-sixth minute Kōji Nakata scored for the Japanese. Chinese players and fans protested that Nakata had pushed the ball with his hand, but the referee allowed the goal. Japan struck once more before the end of regulation play and lifted its third Asian Cup trophy. Furious Chinese fans rioted outside of the stadium.

The 2007 Asian Cup was one for the record books. It was hosted by four nations: Indonesia, Malaysia, Thailand, and Vietnam. Australia participated in the AFC for the first time after leaving the Oceania Football Confederation. Despite the war at home, the Iraqi national team beat Saudi Arabia in the final game, winning its first Asian Cup.

CHAPTER 4

COPA AMÉRICA

The oldest soccer tournament in the world started in 1916 when four teams–Argentina, Brazil, Chile, and Uruguay–decided to play against each other in a tournament. They called this tournament the South American Championship of Nations. The championship has grown considerably since then. In the 1920s it was an annual competition, and between 1940 and the late 1950s it was played unofficially many times in many different formats. In 1975, it was renamed Copa América, which is Spanish for "America Cup." It was agreed that all countries belonging to the Confederación Sudamericana de Fútbol (the South American Football Confederation, or CONMEBOL) would participate in Copa América every four years.

CONMEBOL has ten members: Argentina, Bolivia, Brazil, Chile, Colombia, Ecuador, Paraguay, Peru, Uruguay, and Venezuela. Copa América is an extremely competitive tournament, and seven of these countries have won the cup at least once. The league is dominated by Argentina and Uruguay. Both countries have won fourteen

Argentine midfielder Fernando Redondo (left) *dribbles the ball during a 1993 Copa América match.*

TEAM	TITLES/YEAR
ARGENTINA	14 (1921, 1925, 1927, 1929, 1937, 1941, 1945, 1946, 1947, 1955, 1957, 1959, 1991, 1993)
BOLIVIA	1 (1963)
BRAZIL	8 (1919, 1922, 1949, 1989, 1997, 1999, 2004, 2007)
COLOMBIA	1 (2001)
PARAGUAY	2 (1953, 1979)
PERU	2 (1939, 1975)
URUGUAY	14 (1916, 1917, 1920, 1923, 1924, 1926, 1935, 1942, 1956, 1959, 1967, 1983, 1987, 1995)

titles. This is an especially significant achievement considering that Brazil, the five-time World Cup champ, is also a contender in Copa América. In fact, Brazil has won the cup eight times.

Starting in the 1980s, many European teams began to attract skillful South American players to their ranks. This initiated a massive migration of talented footballers from South America. They joined legendary teams in England, France, Italy, and Spain. This created a huge problem for the South American national teams. Scheduling problems made it difficult for their star players who had joined teams abroad to find the time to play in Copa América. With some of the most important South American players absent, the tournament began to lose some of the prestige that it once enjoyed.

EXPANDING ITS REACH

To renew people's interest in the tournament, CONMEBOL decided in 1993 to begin inviting two teams from other confederations to compete. These teams are drawn mainly from CONCACAF, the sister organization that regulates teams from North America, Central America, and the Caribbean. This idea

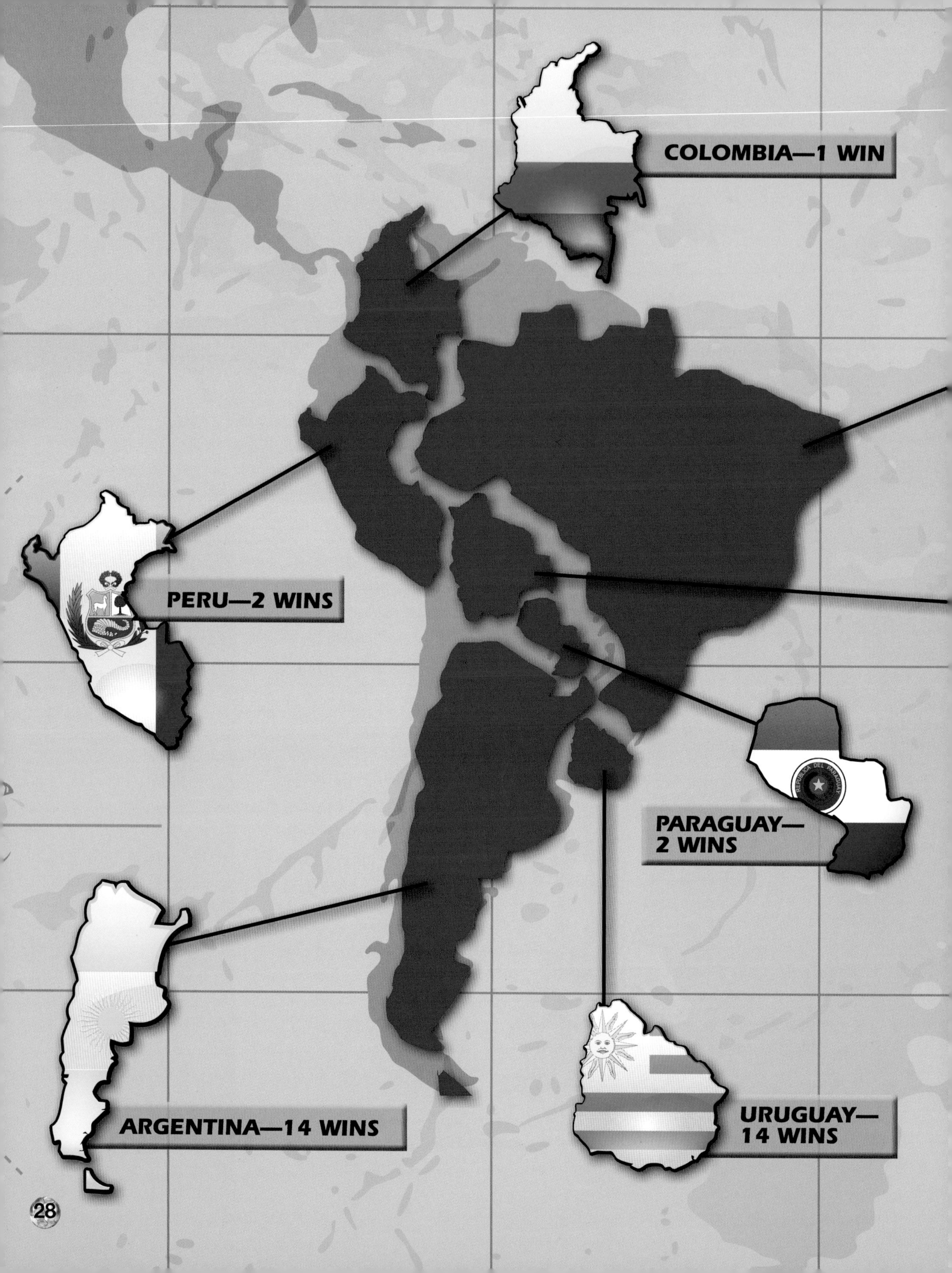
COLOMBIA—1 WIN
PERU—2 WINS
PARAGUAY—
2 WINS
ARGENTINA—14 WINS
URUGUAY—
14 WINS

COPA AMÉRICA

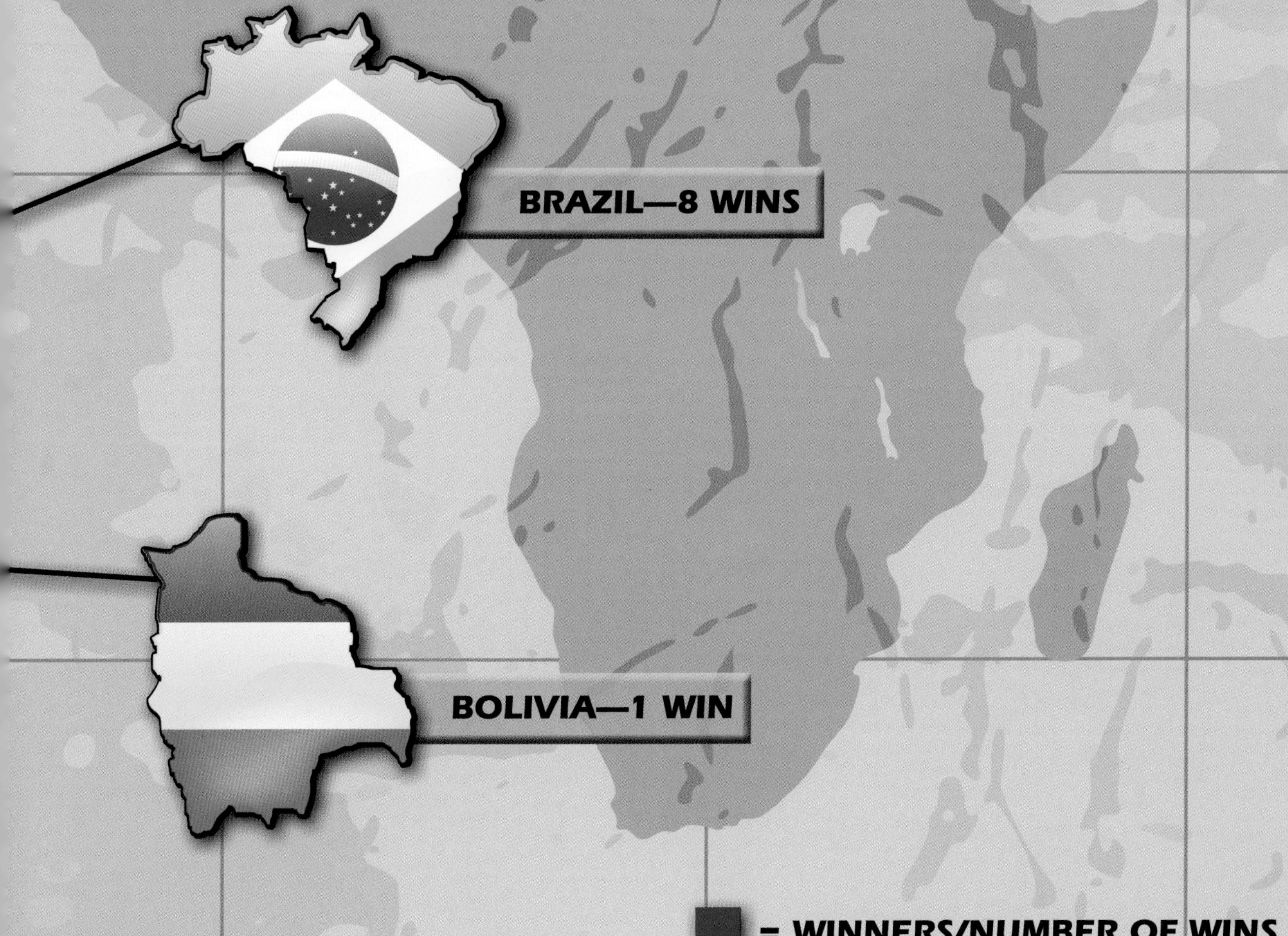

BRAZIL—8 WINS

BOLIVIA—1 WIN

= WINNERS/NUMBER OF WINS

REGION:
SOUTH AMERICA

CONFEDERATION:
CONFEDERACIÓN SUDAMERICANA DE FÚTBOL (CONMEBOL)

PARTICIPATING COUNTRIES:
12

TROPHY:
COPA AMÉRICA TROPHY

The Copa América has become more competitive since additional countries have been invited to participate. Here, Mexico's Francisco Rodriguez (right) tries to stop Uruguay's Maximiliano Pereira (left).

has been a major success. With the addition of countries like Mexico, the United States, and Honduras, the Copa América has regained much of its reputation. It has also become a tournament for the entire Americas.

More importantly, the expansion of the tournament elevated the stakes and the level of competition. This has forced the leading South American teams to call their best players back to the tournament. The final games in the 2004 and 2007 tournaments were classic matches between powerhouses Argentina and Brazil. Ultimately, Brazil became

the back-to-back champion, demonstrating that it was still a force to be reckoned with.

SOUTH AMERICAN STARS

Uruguayan player José Piendibene scored the first goal in Copa América history during the opening match against Chile in 1916. Since then, more than 2,200 goals have been scored in this tournament.

South American players are highly skilled and famous for their ability to control the tempo of the game. They are also known for their spirited style, often improvising and performing spectacular ball tricks. As a result, it is not surprising that some of the most talented players in world soccer have played in the Copa América. Brazilian stars such as Pelé, Rivaldo Vitor Borba Ferreira, and Robson "Robinho" de Souza have all thrilled soccer fans in the Copa América. The most successful team in the Copa América, Argentina, also counts some famous players among its lineup, including Gabriel Batistuta, Martín Palermo, Jorge Burruchaga, and Sergio Goycochea.

Chilean Carlos Caszely was named Best Player in the 1979 cup. Uruguayans Enzo Francescoli and Ruben Sosa were named Best Player in 1989 and 1995, respectively. Peru's 1975 squad included legendary midfielder Teófilo Cubillas. Colombia's superstar Carlos Valderrama delighted fans with his incredible passing skills in 1987, and Paraguay's José Saturnino Cardozo's 1995 goals became legendary. Luis Hernández of Mexico had the honor of scoring the 2,000th goal in the competition in 1997. Two years later, his countryman Miguel Ángel Zepeda scored the 2,100th goal.

CHAPTER 5

THE GOLD CUP

Before the Confederation of North, Central America and Caribbean Association Football (CONCACAF) was founded in 1961, this region was divided into two associations. The first was the Confederación Centroamericana y del Caribe de Fútbol (CCCF), which consisted of Central America and most of the Caribbean. The second was the North American Football Confederation (NAFC), which consisted of Canada, Cuba, Mexico, and the United States. The CCCF held its own championship from 1941 to 1961. The NAFC held only two championships: one in 1947, and one in 1949.

Luis Garcia and Jorge Campos of Mexico lift the Gold Cup after beating Brazil in the 1996 final.

TEAM	*TITLES/YEAR*
CANADA	*2 (1985, 2000)*
COSTA RICA	*3 (1963, 1969, 1989)*
GUATEMALA	*1 (1967)*
HAITI	*1 (1973)*
HONDURAS	*1 (1981)*
MEXICO	*7 (1965, 1971, 1977, 1993, 1996, 1998, 2003)*
UNITED STATES	*4 (1991, 2002, 2005, 2007)*

When CONCACAF combined these two confederations in 1963, the CONCACAF Championship was born.

The CONCACAF Championship had limited success. Mexico and the United States didn't always participate or send their best players. Jack Warner, the CONCACAF president since 1990, decided to overhaul the competition. He renamed it the CONCACAF Gold Cup and gave the United States and Mexico the right to host all the championships to date.

Twenty-six nations competed in the qualifiers for the first tournament, which was held in the United States in 1991. Eight teams reached the finals in Los Angeles and Pasadena, California. The U.S. team won the tournament, but it was the semifinal game against Mexico, its first victory over its neighbors in eleven years, that created the most intense and entertaining rivalry in the Gold Cup.

MEXICO DOMINATES THE FIELD

In 1993, the cup was cohosted by the new soccer rivals. This time Mexico took revenge, defeating the United States 4–0 in front of 120,000 fans in Mexico City's Azteca Stadium. Two years later, the cup was hosted by the United States. This time the field was expanded to encompass nine teams, including Brazil as a guest team. Mexico and the United States did not face each other this time, and Mexico took its second Gold Cup after beating Brazil in the final.

COSTA RICA—
3 WINS
MEXICO—
7 WINS
GUATEMALA—
1 WIN

THE GOLD CUP

REGION:
NORTH AMERICA, CENTRAL AMERICA, AND THE CARIBBEAN

CONFEDERATION
CONFEDERATION OF NORTH, CENTRAL AMERICA AND CARIBBEAN ASSOCIATION FOOTBALL (CONCACAF)

PARTICIPATING COUNTRIES:
12

TROPHY:
GOLD CUP TROPHY

The United States hosted again in 1998, and ten teams participated in the finals. Brazil returned as a guest, but it was the Jamaican team that most fans paid attention to. Jamaica almost reached the final but lost against Mexico in the semifinals. In the other semifinal match, the United States beat Brazil 1–0. This set the stage for another final against Mexico. In front of a Los Angeles crowd of Mexican fans, Mexico won its third straight Gold Cup.

THE UNITED STATES TAKES CONTROL

Twelve teams played in the 2000 Gold Cup. Colombia, Peru, and the Republic of Korea were the guest teams. This time the gold went to Canada. The Canadian team defeated Colombia in the final, giving Canada its first major international soccer honor in more than one hundred years. In 2002, the United States began a dominant run, beating Costa Rica in the final. The United States also won third place in the 2003 match that was once again cohosted with Mexico. This was Mexico's fourth Gold Cup title. The United States advanced to the final again in the 2005 Gold Cup, playing against the Panamanian team, which had made it to the final for the first time in history. It took the United States 120 minutes of intense play and a penalty shoot-out to win its third Gold Cup title.

The 2007 Gold Cup saw the two big rivals back in the final. Mexico struck first with a goal from Andres Guardado, but the United States fought back in the second half. Goals from Landon Donovan and Benny Feilhaber gave the United States its fourth Gold Cup title. The rivalry between the two teams remains strong.

Frankie Hejduk of the United States (right) *battles with Canadian Atiba Hutchinson* (left) *for the ball during a 2007 Gold Cup match in Chicago.*

CHAPTER 6

THE UEFA EUROPEAN FOOTBALL CHAMPIONSHIP

The Union of European Football Associations (UEFA) European Football Championship is the main football competition in Europe. Interestingly, it is also the youngest regional competition in the world. Nevertheless, the EURO (as it is commonly referred to by soccer fans) has been a long time coming.

Henri Delaunay, the president of the French Football Federation, first planned a tournament for European nations in 1927. With the world's attention focused on the emerging World Cup, Delaunay's dream had to wait until 1954. This was the year that the UEFA was created. The first EURO was played in France in 1960, five years after Delaunay's death. In his honor, the trophy was named after him and designed by his son. Seventeen countries participated in the first EURO, with four teams competing in the finals. On July 10, 1960, the Soviet Union beat Yugoslavia in the final match in Paris, becoming the first EURO champion. (The Soviet Union, or USSR, was a Communist republic consisting of Russia and more than a dozen neighboring countries. It existed from 1922 to 1991.)

Twenty-nine countries participated in the next EURO, held in 1964 in Spain. In the semifinals, the defending champions defeated Denmark 3–0, and Spain beat Hungary in overtime. For political reasons, Spain had refused to play the Soviet Union in the 1960 EURO semifinals. This time Spain was playing at home. Spain defeated the Soviets in front of more than seventy-nine thousand fans in Madrid, winning its first European championship. Four years later, the EURO traveled to Italy. Thirty-three nations fought for four final spots. As in 1964, the host team became the champion. But it

Spanish midfielder Xavi Hernandez celebrates after scoring against Russia in the 2008 UEFA semifinal.

TEAM	TITLES / YEAR
CZECHOSLOVAKIA	1 (1976)
DENMARK	1 (1992)
FRANCE	2 (1984, 2000)
GERMANY *	3 (1972, 1980, 1996)
GREECE	1 (2004)
ITALY	1 (1968)
NETHERLANDS	1 (1988)
SPAIN	2 (1964, 2008)
USSR	1 (1960)

* WEST GERMANY WON THE 1972 AND 1980 UEFA TITLES

wasn't easy for Italy. After tying Yugoslavia in the final game, Italy had to play a second match, two days later, to decide the winner.

GERMAN DOMINATION

In the 1970s, West Germany became the first team to play in three consecutive EURO finals, wining two of them. The first title came in a thrilling 1972 game against the Soviet Union. Star striker Gerd Müller scored two goals, clinching the game for the Germans. The Germans were runners-up in EURO 1976 in Yugoslavia, losing the final game in a penalty shoot-out against Czechoslovakia.

The plucky Germans managed to come back to win the title in EURO 1980 in Italy. The hero of the match was Germany's Horst Hrubesch, who scored the two goals that gave Germany its second EURO trophy.

As the host of the EURO 1988, Germany was a clear favorite to win. However, the team was unable to overcome the dynamic Dutch team commanded by Marco van Basten. The Dutch knocked the Germans out of the tournament in the semifinals. The Netherlands went on to win the tournament with an amazing looping volley from van Basten against the Soviet Union.

Germany reached the final for a record fourth time in 1992, only to be defeated by Denmark. Denmark had not qualified to participate in the tournament but was selected to take the place of

UEFA EUROPEAN FOOTBALL CHAMPIONSHIP

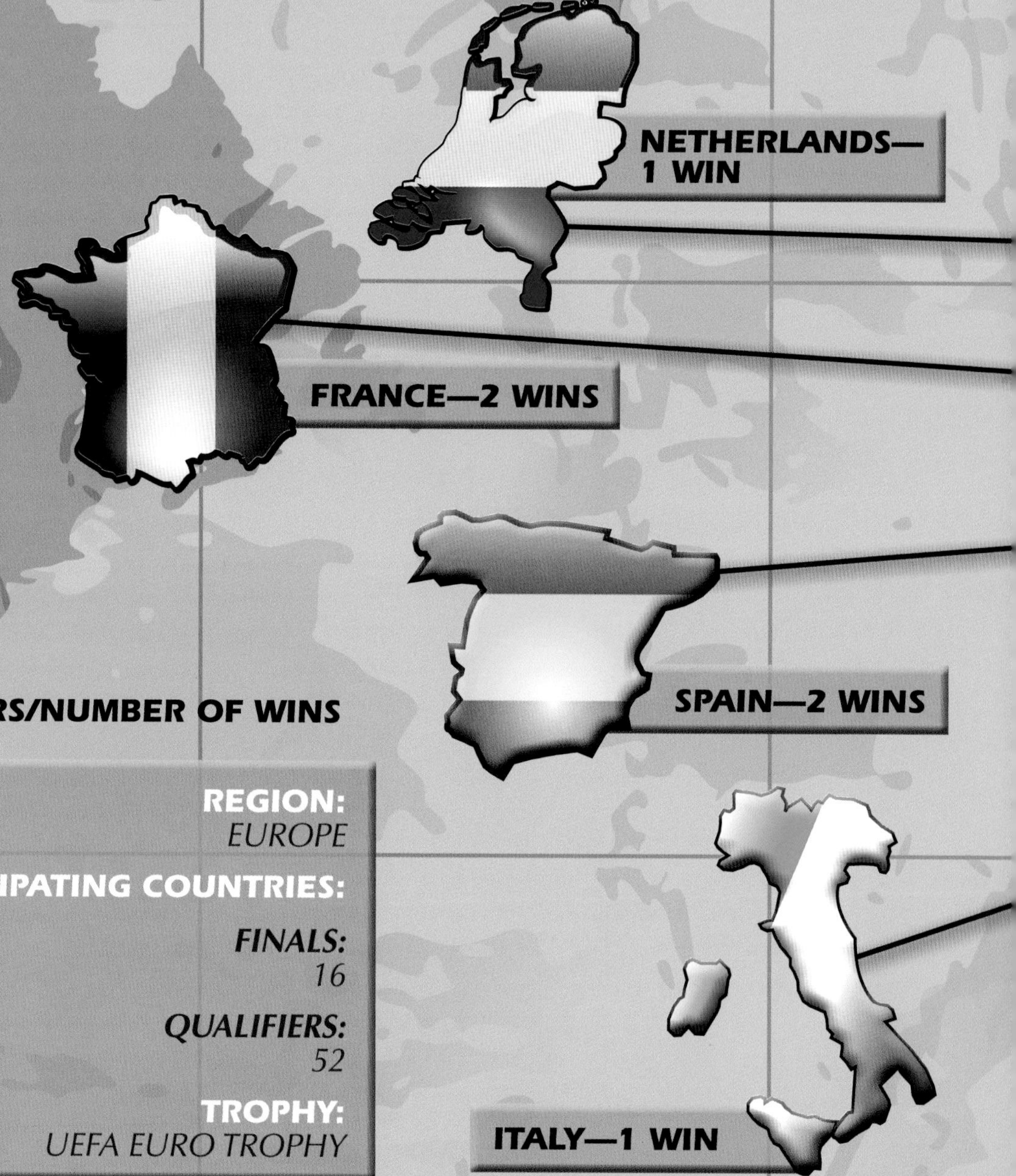

NETHERLANDS—1 WIN

FRANCE—2 WINS

SPAIN—2 WINS

ITALY—1 WIN

= WINNERS/NUMBER OF WINS

REGION:
EUROPE

PARTICIPATING COUNTRIES:

FINALS:
16

QUALIFIERS:
52

TROPHY:
UEFA EURO TROPHY

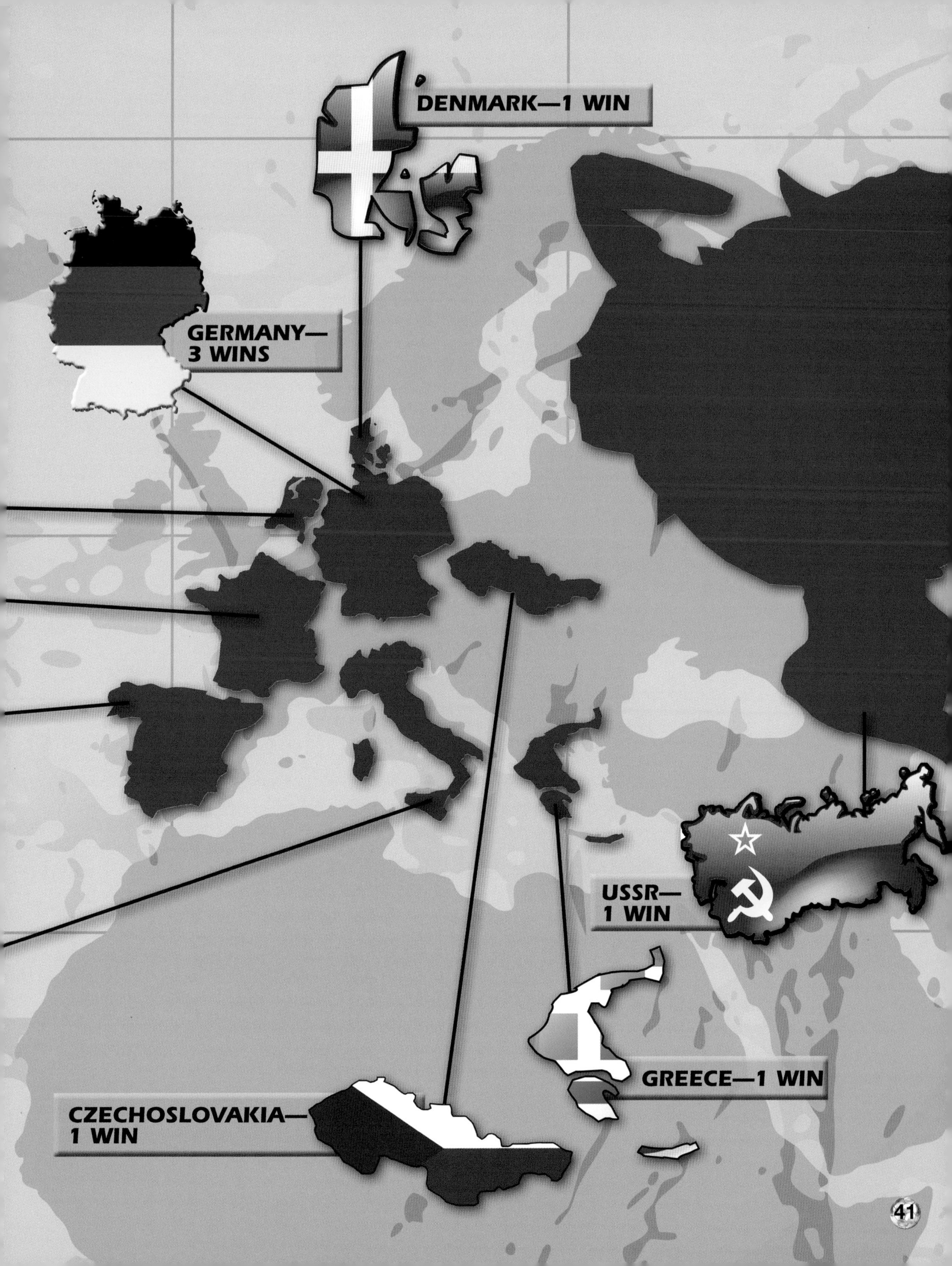
DENMARK—1 WIN
GERMANY—
3 WINS
USSR—
1 WIN
GREECE—1 WIN
CZECHOSLOVAKIA—
1 WIN

German striker Oliver Bierhoff scores a goal during the EURO 1996 tournament. Germany has won more EUROs than any other country.

Yugoslavia. Yugoslavia did not participate in the tournament because of a civil war, which lasted until 2001. After the war, Yugoslavia broke apart, becoming several different countries. The Danish team beat Germany by a score of 2–0 in Gothenburg, Sweden.

Germany returned to the final four years later in EURO 1996 in England. This time the Germans faced the Czech Republic. After ninety minutes of tense soccer, the game ended in a 1–1 tie. Oliver Bierhoff scored his second goal of the night in overtime, giving Germany its third EURO title.

A NEW ERA IN EUROPEAN SOCCER

The 2004 EURO in Portugal was a tournament full of surprises. Germany, Italy, and Spain didn't advance beyond the group stage. France, the EURO 2000 champion, was eliminated by Greece in the quarterfinals. The two countries that advanced to the EURO final–Greece and Portugal–had never made it to the EURO final before. Greece won the match in front of sixty thousand incredulous Portuguese fans in Lisbon's Estádio da Luz. Greece's EURO victory was a real upset, considering that the team had also never won a match in its previous tournaments.

The EURO 2008 was hosted by Austria and Switzerland, the second time that two countries have shared the honor. Greece, the defending champion, did not win a single

game and went home after the group stage. The two host countries suffered the same fate. On the other hand, Spain had one of the most remarkable tournaments in recent history, going undefeated to the final against Germany to win its second EURO championship title.

EUROPEAN LEGENDS

Many legendary players have had their best performances while playing at the EURO competition. Frenchman Michel Platini currently leads the pack with nine goals in five matches during the EURO 1984. Platini delighted soccer fans all over the world by scoring two "perfect" hat tricks (one header and one goal with each foot) during the tournament. He won the cup for France in a thrilling final game against Spain.

Dutch striker Marco van Basten never had a chance to shine during World Cup competition, but the "Flying Dutchman" came off the bench at the EURO 1988 to score a hat trick against England. In the second game against Germany, van Basten scored two minutes before the end of the game to win it for the Dutch. The Dutch team faced off against the USSR in the final. In the fifty-fourth minute of the game, van Basten put a volley past the Soviet goalie. This amazing goal gave the Dutch team its first major international title in history.

Endurance and consistency are important qualities for the greatest players, and six men have written their names in EURO history by participating in four tournaments. EURO winner in 1980, Lothar Matthäus led the German defense in 1980, 1984, and 1988, and remarkably returned in 2000. Two extraordinary goalies have played four consecutive EURO Cups: Danish legend Peter Schmeichel (1988, 1992, 1996, and 2000) and Dutch superstar Edwin van der Sar (1996, 2000, 2004, and 2008). Dutch midfielder Aron Winter participated in 1988, 1992, 1996, and 2000. French defender Lilian Thuram has played in four EURO tournaments, winning in 2000. He also holds the record for the most appearances at the championship, with sixteen games played. This exclusive list also includes Italian wonder Alessandro Del Piero, who played in 1996, 2000, 2004, and 2008.

CHAPTER 7

THE WOMEN'S WORLD CUP

Women's soccer teams were formed in England as early as 1895. In the early twentieth century, British women joined the workforce while the men fought in World War I. Women who worked in munitions factories formed soccer teams, and their games began attracting considerable crowds.

Several attempts were made to organize an international women's tournament, including a women's committee formed by UEFA in 1971. However, this did not happen until 1983, when FIFA followed the UEFA in creating a committee for women's soccer. FIFA decided that the first Women's World Cup would be played in China in 1991. The inaugural tournament was a major success. More than sixty-five thousand people watched the United States claim victory over Norway in China's Tianhe Stadium. The second tournament was held in Sweden in 1995, where the Norwegian team won the championship for the first time.

American player Brandi Chastain celebrates during the 1999 Women's World Cup. Chastain scored the penalty kick that won the championship for the United States.

YEAR/HOST	WINNER	FINAL SCORE	RUNNER-UP
1991 CHINA	UNITED STATES	2–1	NORWAY
1995 SWEDEN	NORWAY	2–0	GERMANY
1999 UNITED STATES	UNITED STATES	0–0 (5–4) *	CHINA
2003 UNITED STATES	GERMANY	2–1	SWEDEN
2007 CHINA	GERMANY	2–0	BRAZIL

* GAME DECIDED IN A PENALTY SHOOT-OUT

Norway's Ann Kristin Aarønes claimed the Golden Shoe Award, and teammate Hege Riise won the Golden Ball Award.

RISING POPULARITY

The popularity of women's soccer was confirmed when it was included for the first time in the 1996 Atlanta Olympic Games. The 1996 games brought a great deal of attention to women's soccer, but it was the 1999 World Cup, hosted by the United States, that brought the popularity of the game to a new level. Sixteen teams played in eight U.S. cities, capturing the imagination of American soccer fans. Crowds showed up in the stadiums in record numbers. The final game between the United States and China, held at the Rose Bowl in Pasadena, California, was the most attended women's sports event in U.S. history. More than ninety thousand women's soccer fans packed the stadium. The game remained scoreless after overtime and was ultimately decided in a tense penalty shoot-out. More than forty million people around the world were watching on television when American midfielder Brandi Chastain scored the tournament-winning penalty, ultimately giving the host team its second World Cup title.

GERMAN DOMINATION

The 2003 Women's World Cup was originally scheduled to take place in China. However, an outbreak of severe acute respiratory

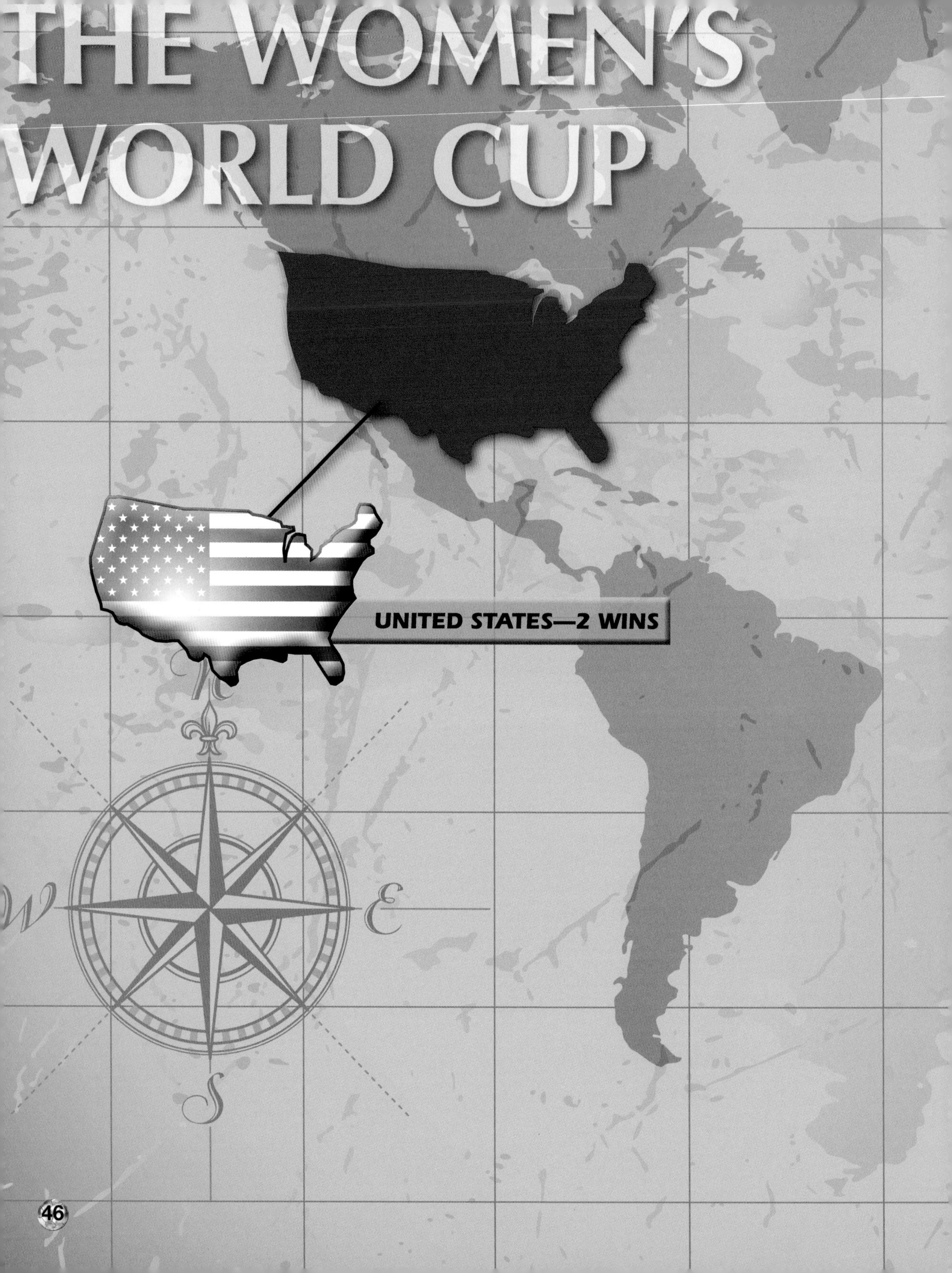
THE WOMEN'S
WORLD CUP
UNITED STATES—2 WINS
W
E
S

GERMANY—2 WINS

= WINNERS/NUMBER OF WINS

REGION:
WORLDWIDE

PARTICIPATING COUNTRIES:
16

TROPHY:
FIFA WOMEN'S WORLD CUP TROPHY

syndrome (SARS) in China forced FIFA to move the tournament to the United States. The tournament was filled with many exciting moments. Germany defeated Sweden in the championship, and the German coach, Tina Theune-Meyer, became the first female coach to lead a team to victory in the Women's World Cup.

Four years later, the cup returned to China. Germany once again claimed the championship after beating Brazil in the final. Germany became the first women's team to win back-to-back tournaments, but it was Brazilian striker Marta who captured the attention of soccer fans across the globe with her fantastic skills and free-flowing style.

FEMALE STARS

In the history of soccer, the achievements of players like America's Mia Hamm, Germany's Birgit Prinz, and Brazil's Marta can be ranked alongside those of legends such as Pelé, Maradona, Cruyff, and Beckenbauer. Mia Hamm is perhaps most responsible for the recent explosion of interest in the Women's World Cup. Born in Alabama, at fifteen years of age Hamm became the youngest player to join the U.S. women's national team. By the age of nineteen, she was the youngest member of the U.S. squad that won the 1991 World Cup in China. She was FIFA World Soccer Player of the Year in 2001 and 2002 and during her career drew the biggest crowds of any player. At the 1999 U.S. Women's World Cup, Hamm scored two goals in the first round and one penalty in the final shoot-out, giving the U.S. women's national team its second World Cup.

Brazilian star Marta (right) *dribbles away from two French defenders during the 2003 Women's World Cup.*

CHAPTER 8

YOUTH SOCCER WORLD CUPS

Although almost every country on the planet participates in the World Cup, not many nations have the opportunity to advance beyond the qualifying rounds. Even fewer have the costly infrastructure required to host such a large sporting event. Because of this, soccer federations around the world grew concerned that the World Cup would become an elitist sport.

FIFA's answer to this problem was the creation of age-specific international tournaments. Imitating the structure and rules of the World Cup, these tournaments bring the game to fans in countries around the world. Youth Soccer World Cups are very successful, and fans enjoy getting to see young and promising players, the ones that will become the stars of tomorrow, engaged in serious competition.

Mexico's Julio Domínguez (left) and Argentina's Sergio Agüero (right) fight for the ball during the 2007 U-20 World Cup in Canada.

PERFORMANCE BY COUNTRY U-17

TEAM	TITLES/YEAR
BRAZIL	3 (1997, 1999, 2003)
FRANCE	1 (2001)
GHANA	2 (1991, 1995)
MEXICO	1 (2005)
NIGERIA	3 (1985, 1993, 2007)
SAUDI ARABIA	1 (1989)
USSR	1 (1987)

PERFORMANCE BY COUNTRY U-20

TEAM	TITLES/YEAR
ARGENTINA	6 (1979, 1995, 1997, 2001, 2005, 2007)
BRAZIL	4 (1983, 1985, 1993, 2003)
GERMANY	1 (1981)
PORTUGAL	2 (1989, 1991)
SPAIN	1 (1999)
USSR	1 (1977)
YUGOSLAVIA	1 (1987)

THE U-17 WORLD CUP: AFRICAN DOMINANCE

With the exception of Brazil and France, the victorious nations in the U-17 World Cup don't come from Europe or South America, the continents that have traditionally dominated world soccer. Ghana, Mexico, Nigeria, Saudi Arabia, and the Soviet Union have seen their youth teams achieve victory. On top of this, countries that are not traditionally known for their soccer teams, like China, New Zealand, and Trinidad and Tobago, have had the opportunity to host thrilling and successful soccer events.

The leading teams in the U-17 cup are Brazil, Ghana, and Nigeria. The fact that two African countries have been so dominant in the U-17 World Cup is good news for international soccer.

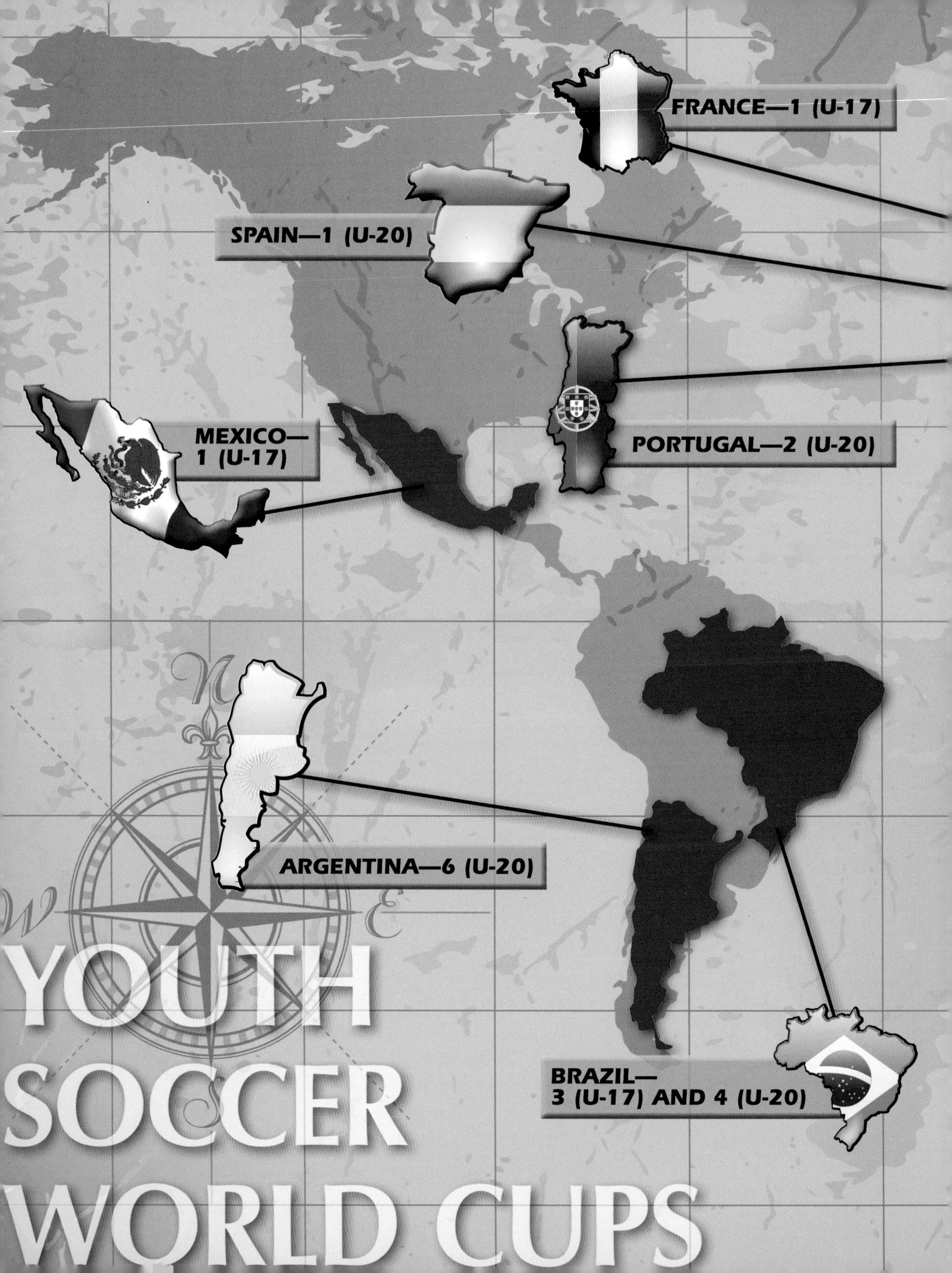
FRANCE—1 (U-17)
SPAIN—1 (U-20)
PORTUGAL—2 (U-20)
MEXICO—
1 (U-17)
ARGENTINA—6 (U-20)
BRAZIL—
3 (U-17) AND 4 (U-20)
YOUTH
SOCCER
WORLD CUPS

GERMANY—1 (U-20)

YUGOSLAVIA 1 (U-20)

USSR—1 (U-17) AND 1 (U-20)

= WINNERS

NIGERIA—
3 (U-17)

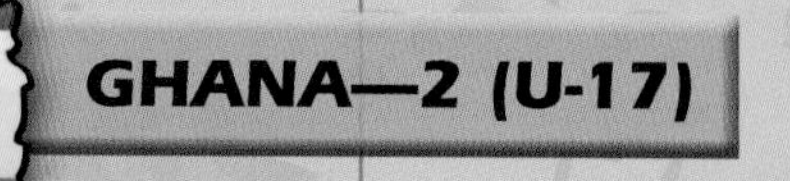

GHANA—2 (U-17)

REGION:
WORLDWIDE

CATEGORIES:
U-17—PLAYERS UNDER THE AGE OF SEVENTEEN

U-20—PLAYERS UNDER THE AGE OF TWENTY

TROPHY:
FIFA U-17 WORLD CUP TROPHY

FIFA U-20 WORLD CUP TROPHY

However, there has been controversy surrounding some African teams. Several soccer federations have alleged that some players on these teams are older than reported. FIFA has worked extensively to solve this problem, and as the U-17 has become more organized these rumors have faded. Moving past this controversy, African nations have continued to excel in the U-17 cup. History was made in the 1993 U-17 World Cup in Japan when Nigeria and Ghana played each other for the first all-African World Cup final.

THE U-20 WORLD CUP: CENTER STAGE

By the time players participate in the U-20 world championship, many of them have already been pegged as promising young athletes. Some are even the stars of their clubs and national teams. The U-20 Cup showcases emerging nations' soccer stars, allowing players under the age of twenty to step into the spotlight of international soccer.

Formerly known as the FIFA World Youth Championship, the U-20 Cup has been played every two years since its creation in 1977. Argentina, with six championships, is the most successful nation to play in the U-20 World Cup. It is followed by Brazil, which has four championships. European countries that have performed well in U-20 competitions include Portugal (a two-time champion), Germany, the Soviet Union, Spain, and Yugoslavia. The U-20 cup has never been won by an African nation, but Ghana and Nigeria have made it to two finals each. Japan, Mexico, and Qatar have also made it to the finals. As with the U-17 tournament, the U-20 World Cup has been hosted by countries that are

Nigeria's Ademola Rafeal (in white) drives the ball through a group of Spanish defenders in the 2007 U-17 World Cup. Nigeria has won more U-17 World Cup titles than any other country.

not yet established soccer powerhouses, such as Australia, Canada, Malaysia, and Qatar.

More than one million fans attended the 2007 U-20 World Cup, which was held in Canada. This broke all previous attendance records for youth soccer. The tournament was also significant for Argentina's team, which won the championship. It was the second back-to-back victory for Argentina. Players like Argentinean Sergio "Kun" Agüero (winner of the cup's Golden Shoe) U.S. sensation Josmer Altidore, and Mexican superstar and former U-17 world champion Giovani Dos Santos were among the upcoming soccer celebrities that played in Canada. These players define the kind of talent that will illuminate the world of international soccer in the future.

GLOSSARY

apartheid A social system, once practiced in South Africa, that enforced racial segregation. Apartheid was grossly unfair to South Africa's black population, and the human rights abuses that took place under apartheid made the nation unpopular with the international community. South Africa ended apartheid in the early 1990s.

committee A group of people in charge of performing a job.

consecutive Two or more things that occur in succession.

dominate To show force or superiority.

epic Something that is heroic and impressive.

Fair Play Award An honor awarded to a player or team who shows good sportsmanship during a competition.

Fédération Internationale de Football Association (FIFA) FIFA is the world governing body of international soccer. It oversees the world's major soccer tournaments, including the World Cup.

Golden Ball Award An honor presented to the best player at each World Cup final.

Golden Shoe Award An honor presented to the top scorer of the World Cup.

infrastructure The basic facilities and services needed for organizing a sporting event, such as stadiums and transportation.

munitions Artillery, such as bullets and missiles.

penalty shoot-out A system of determining a winner in a match that would have otherwise ended in a draw.

qualifiers The round of games that teams play to have the right to participate in a tournament.

red card A card shown by a referee to a player to indicate that the player is being ejected from the game.

severe acute respiratory syndrome (SARS) A respiratory disease that caused a brief epidemic in 2002 and 2003.

umbrella organization An association, or group, of institutions that work together to coordinate activities.

Yugoslav Wars A series of violent conflicts that occurred in the former Socialist Federal Republic of Yugoslavia. The Yugoslav Wars took place between 1991 and 2001 and resulted in the breakup of Yugoslavia into several autonomous states.

FOR MORE INFORMATION

American Youth Soccer Organization
National Support and Training Center
12501 S. Isis Avenue
Hawthorne, CA 90250
(800) 872-2976
Web site: http://soccer.org/home.aspx
This organization administers youth recreational soccer leagues all over the country.

Canadian Soccer Association
Place Soccer Canada
237 rue Metcalfe Street
Ottawa, ON K2P 1R2
Canada
(613) 237-7678
Web site: http://www.canadasoccer.com
The Canadian Soccer Association works to promote soccer and to improve the game at both the national and international levels.

CONCACAF
725 Fifth Avenue, Floor 17
New York, NY 10022
(212) 308-0044
Web site: http://www.concacaf.com
The Confederation of North, Central America and Caribbean Association Football (CONCACAF) oversees soccer in its forty member countries. It is one of six divisions of FIFA.

National Soccer Hall of Fame
18 Stadium Circle
Oneonta, NY 13820
(607) 432-3351
Web site: http://www.soccerhall.org

The National Soccer Hall of Fame preserves and promotes the history of soccer in the United States.

The Ontario Soccer Association
7601 Martin Grove Road
Vaughan, ON L4L 9E4
Canada
(905) 264-9390
Web site: http://www.ontariosoccer.net/home.aspx
The Ontario Soccer Association organizes and promotes soccer at both the regional and national levels.

U.S. Soccer Federation
1801 S. Prairie Avenue
Chicago, IL 60616
(312) 808-1300
Web site: http://www.ussoccer.com
The U.S. Soccer Federation oversees both professional and amateur soccer and helps to promote and develop the sport.

WEB SITES

Due to the changing nature of Internet links, Rosen Publishing has developed an online list of Web sites related to the subject of this book. This site is updated regularly. Please use this link to access the list:

http://www.rosenlinks.com/wsb/tour

FOR FURTHER READING

Buckley, James. *Pelé*. New York, NY: DK Children, 2007.

Buxton, Ted. *Soccer Skills: For Young Players*. Richmond Hill, ON, Canada: Firefly Books, 2007.

DK Publishing. *Soccer: The Ultimate Guide*. New York, NY: DK Children, 2008.

Esckilsen, Erik. *Offsides*. New York, NY: Houghton Mifflin Books for Children, 2004.

Fitzgerald, Dawn. *Soccer Chick Rules*. New York, NY: Square Fish, 2007.

Gifford, Clive. *The Kingfisher Soccer Encyclopedia*. New York, NY: Kingfisher, 2006.

Goldblatt, David. *The Ball Is Round: A Global History of Soccer*. New York, NY: Riverhead, 2008.

Hamm, Mia. *Go for the Goal: A Champion's Guide to Winning in Soccer and Life*. New York, NY: Quill, 2000.

Hornby, Hugh. *Soccer*. New York, NY: DK Children, 2008.

Hunt, Chris. *The Complete Book of Soccer*. Buffalo, NY: Firefly Books, 2006.

Rigby, Robert. *Goal!: The Dream Begins*. New York, NY: Harcourt Paperbacks, 2006.

Stewart, Barbara, and Pam Whitesnell. *Women's Soccer: The Passionate Game*. Vancouver, BC, Canada: Greystone Books, 2003.

Stewart, Mark. *The World Cup*. New York, NY: Franklin Watts (Scholastic), 2003.

Wangerin, David. *Soccer in a Football World: The Story of America's Forgotten Game*. Philadelphia, PA: Temple University Press, 2008.

Whitfield, David. *World Cup*. New York, NY: Weigl Publishers, 2007.

Wilson, Jonathan. *Inverting the Pyramid: The History of Football Tactics*. London, England: Orion, 2008.

Wingate, Brian. *Soccer: Rules, Tips, Strategy, and Safety*. New York, NY: The Rosen Publishing Group, 2007.

BIBLIOGRAPHY

Crouch, Terry. *The World Cup: The Complete History.* London, England: Aurum Press, Ltd., 2006.

Expertfootball.com. "Soccer Styles of Play." Retrieved February 28, 2009 (http://expertfootball.com/coaching/styles.php).

FIFA.com. "The History of FIFA." Retrieved February 28, 2009 (http://www.fifa.com/classicfootball/history/fifa/historyfifa1.html).

FIFA.com. "Previous FIFA World Cups." Retrieved February 22, 2009 (http://www.fifa.com/worldcup/archive/index.html).

Fiore, Fernando. *The World Cup: The Ultimate Guide to the Greatest Sports Spectacle in the World.* New York, NY: HarperCollins Publishers, 2006.

Hunt, Chris. *The Complete Book of Soccer.* Buffalo, NY: Firefly Books, 2006.

Lisi, Clemente Angelo. *A History of the World Cup: 1930–2006.* Lanham, MD: Scarecrow Press, 2007.

Miers, Charles, and Elio Trifari, eds. *Soccer!: The Game and the World Cup.* New York, NY: Rizzoli International Publications, 1994.

Platini, Michel. "Quotes." MichelPlatini.org. Retrieved March 3, 2009 (http://www.michelplatini.org/Quotes.html).

Radnedge, Keir. *The Complete Encyclopedia of Soccer.* London, England: Carlton Books, 2000.

Weiland, Matt, and Sean Wilsey, eds. *The Thinking Fan's Guide to the World Cup.* New York, NY: HarperCollins Publishers, 2006.

INDEX

ABOUT THE AUTHOR

Mauricio Velázquez de León is a writer and editor living in New York City. A passionate soccer fan, he has attended two World Cups, as well as many international matches featuring players like Beckenbauer, Butragueño, Maradona, Pelé, Platini, and Hugo Sánchez.

PHOTO CREDITS

Cover, p. 1 (top) Paul Gilham/Getty Images; cover, p. 1 (bottom) Franck Fife/AFP/Getty Images; p. 5 Cris Bournocle/AFP/Getty Images; p. 6 Popperfoto/Getty Images; p. 11 Alex Livesey/Getty Images; p. 12 Lefty Shivambu/Gallo Images/Getty Images; p. 14 Issouf Sanogo/AFP/Getty Images; pp. 18, 20, 32, 36, 54 © AP Images; p. 24 Bay Ismoyo/AFP/Getty Images; p. 26 Daniel Garcia/AFP/Getty Images; p. 30 Juan Barreto/AFP/Getty Images; p. 38 Joe Klamar/AFP/Getty Images; p. 42 Gerry Penny/AFP/Getty Images; p. 44 Hector Mata/AFP/Getty Images; p. 48 Tim Sloan/AFP/Getty Images; p. 50 Phillip MacCallum/Getty Images; page backgrounds and borders © www.istockphoto.com/Roberta Casaliggi.

Designer: Matthew Cauli; Photo Researcher: Cindy Reiman